P9-CEL-526

SHIPS

Philip Wilkinson

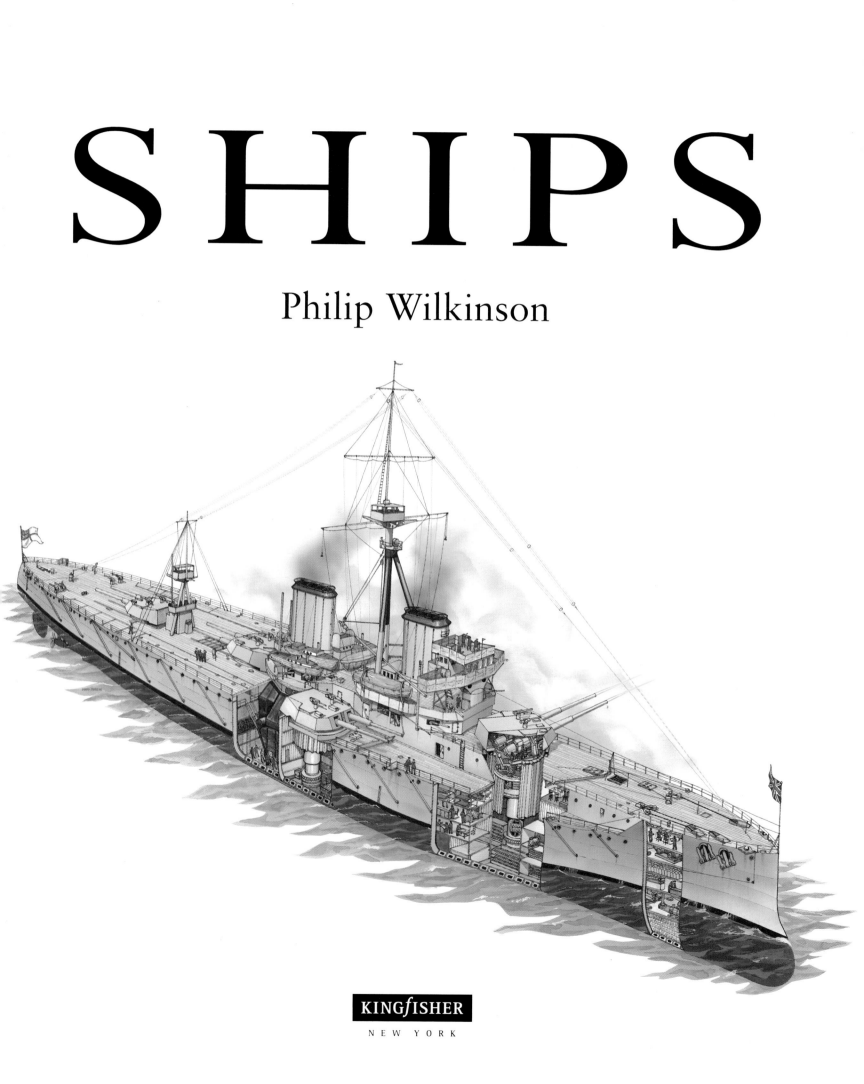

KINGFISHER
NEW YORK

Editor: Julie Ferris
Art director: Mike Davis
Consultant: Dr. Peter Marsden
Production controller: Jacquie Horner
DTP coordinator: Nicky Studdart
Picture manager: Jane Lambert
Proofreader: Sheila Clewley
Cover illustration: David O'Connor
Indexer: Sue Lightfoot

KINGFISHER
Larousse Kingfisher Chambers Inc.
95 Madison Avenue
New York, New York 10016

First published in 2000
10 9 8 7 6 5 4 3 2 1
1TR/0400/SIN/MA/157MA

Copyright © Kingfisher Publications Plc 2000
Text copyright © Philip Wilkinson

All rights reserved under International and Pan-American
Copyright Conventions

LIBRARY OF CONGRESS CATALOGING-IN-PUBLICATION DATA
has been applied for.

ISBN 0-7534-5280-4

The Publisher would like to thank the
National Maritime Museum, London,
for their help and cooperation in the
production of this book.

Printed in Hong Kong

CONTENTS

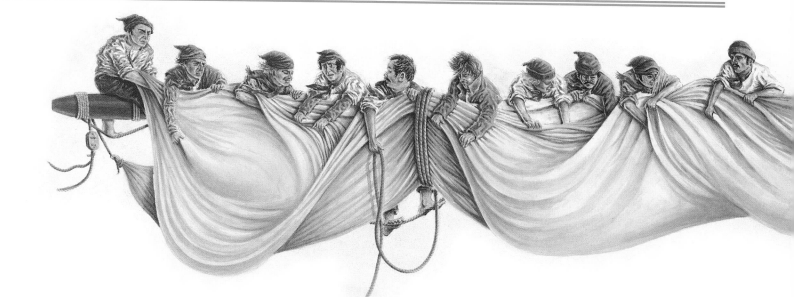

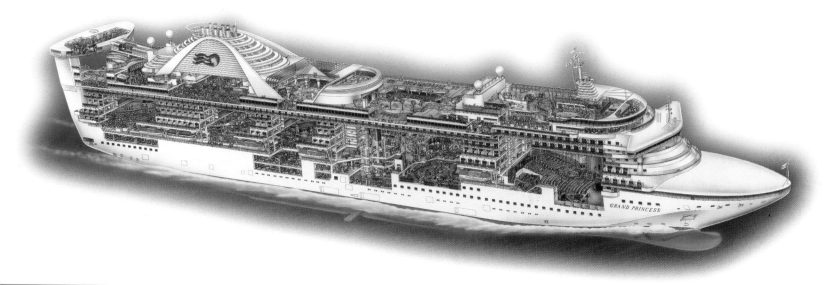

INTRODUCING SHIPS

From the earliest times, people have sailed the oceans, building a huge variety of ships for trade, for war, and for travel across unknown bodies of water to new lands. Ships can be powered by oars, sails, steam, or diesel engines; they can have the elegant wooden structure of a galleon or the tough steel hull of a battleship. All have fascinating stories—tales of bravery, inventiveness, and mastery of the seas.

The best ships

Some ships are successful because of their speed, like the clippers of the 1800s. Others, like Viking longships, succeed because they adapt well to harsh conditions. Many catch the eye with their beauty, while others impress with their sheer size. From awesome galleys and battleships, to elegant clippers and men-of-war, The best of them all combine speed, strength, and seaworthiness—the ability to sail well in any conditions.

A mighty liner

The enormous 80,000-ton French ship *Normandie* was one of the fastest ocean liners at the time. Powerful turboelectric engines gave the ship impressive speed—it crossed the Atlantic Ocean in just four days and three hours in 1935. The tugs in the harbor of New York look tiny next to the ship's huge hull.

TRADE AND DISCOVERY

From the small trading boats of the ancient Egyptians, to the huge container ships of today, merchant ships have penetrated the world's seas. For much of history, traders were also explorers. Braving cold, stormy conditions in tiny ships, they searched for better routes and new sources of goods to buy and sell.

The ancient Egyptians' small sailing boats traveled up and down the Nile River.

The Phoenicians developed the galley, which was powered by oars and a sail.

Ancient Greek ships traded around the Mediterranean Sea.

The Romans moved goods around their large empire in ships with two square sails.

The Vikings explored the North Atlantic in their longships.

Chinese junks could carry tons of cargo in their hulls.

Explorers sailed in small carracks in the 1400s.

East Indiamen traded between Europe, the Far East, and India.

NORTH AMERICA

John Cabot explored Canada

Silver

Tobacco

Columbus sailed in the Santa Maria

EQUATOR

Coffee

SOUTH AMERICA

Magellan sailed around the world

Magellan 1519–1521	→
Dias 1487–1488	→
Da Gama 1497–1499	→
Cook 1768–1779	→
Columbus 1492–1504	→
Cabot 1497–1498	→
Barents 1596–1597	→

Clippers were built for speed.

Steamships meant sailors no longer had to rely on the wind

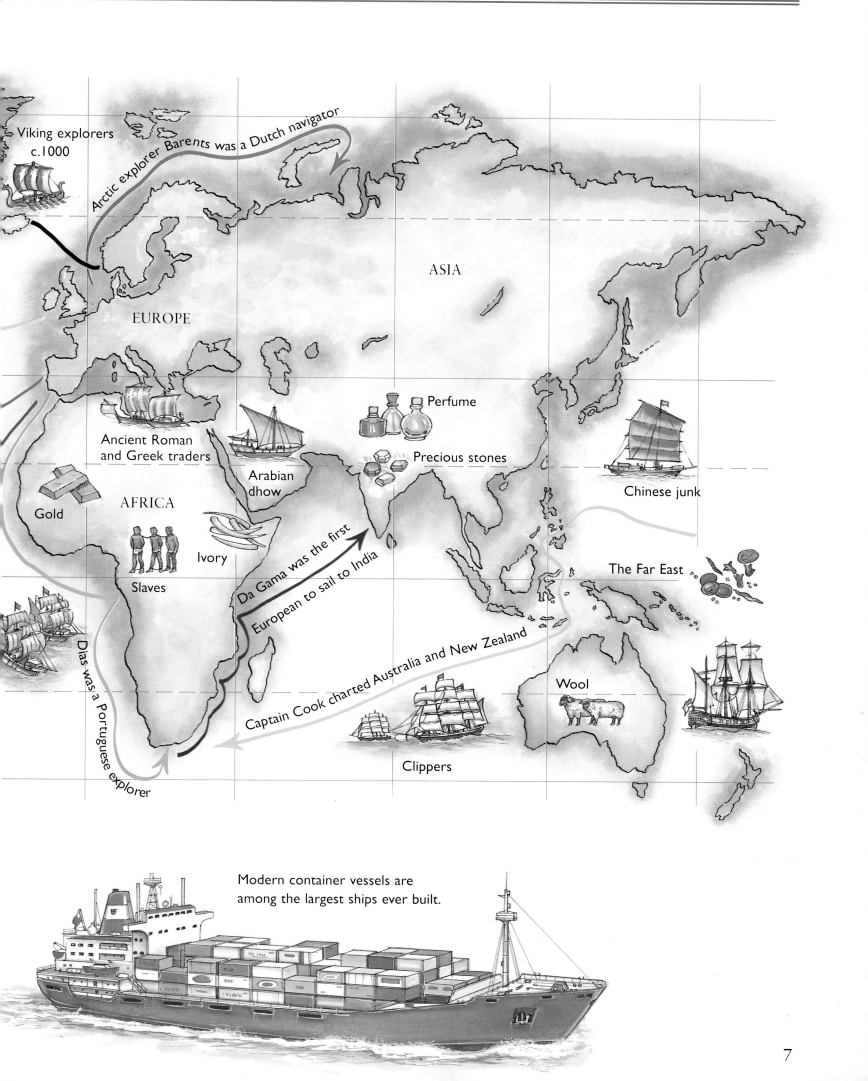

Viking explorers
c.1000

Arctic explorer Barents was a Dutch navigator

ASIA

EUROPE

Perfume

Ancient Roman
and Greek traders

Arabian
dhow

Precious stones

Chinese junk

Gold

AFRICA

Ivory

Da Gama was the first
European to sail to India

The Far East

Slaves

Dias was a Portuguese explorer

Captain Cook charted Australia and New Zealand

Wool

Clippers

Modern container vessels are
among the largest ships ever built.

Viking merchants

The trading vessels used by the Vikings were clinker-built ships (made of overlapping planks) secured with iron nails and strengthened with cross beams. They were wide ships, with room for several tons of cargo. The cargo was stored in the middle of the ship, and covered with animal hides to protect it from the weather. The crew stood on the small decks fore and aft working the sail and controlling the rudder.

Sun compass

Viking sailors used this wooden dial to help find their way. They lined up one of the notches with a point on the horizon directly below the sun at noon. This showed them which direction was south. The pointer was used to set the ship's course.

Rudder

Oar port

Sails were made of canvas or leather

Mainmast

Early traders

Greek trader

The sea was a vital highway in the ancient world. Early civilizations like the Phoenicians, Greeks, and Vikings lived mainly along the coastline. They took to the sea to trade, sailing from one port to the next, but always keeping close to the shore. They usually went out into the more dangerous waters of the Atlantic Ocean during the less stormy summer months. Their trading ships were not fast, relying mainly the wind power, but they were compact and sturdy enough for traveling in treacherous northern seas.

Phoenician traders

In their homeland in Lebanon and Syria, the Phoenicians used high quality cedar wood to make small, sturdy ships. They traded all around the Mediterranean and the Black Sea.

Ancient Rome

The ancient Romans used small, twin-sail vessels for trading. These were usually made from pine or cypress boards, which were attached to an oak frame with wooden pegs.

Trading far and wide

From their homes in Scandinavia, the Vikings traded all over Europe. They dealt in everything from timber and ivory to furs and glassware.

Foredeck

Ships of the East

The people of China and the Muslim countries of the Middle East built unique ships blending their cultural tastes with traditional shipbuilding. Their ships were beautifully built vessels, with hulls and rigging that were well-designed for the local waters. In some ways, these ships were more advanced than those of the West. For example, the shipbuilders of China fitted rudders on the stern—or back—of their large, oceangoing junks about 1,000 years before the rudder appeared in the West.

Arabian dhows
Traders in the Middle East sailed dhows—sleek vessels with one or two masts. Still widely used today, dhows are rigged with lateen (triangular) sails that enable them to sail fast with the wind.

Chinese junks
In the 1300s and the 1400s, the Chinese sent out expeditions to explore the Far East and the Pacific Ocean. The junks used by these Chinese navigators were large, flat-bottomed vessels with a high stern and square bow. Similar vessels still sail off the coasts of China today. The hull of a junk is very strong because it is divided by a series of cross walls called bulkheads. The bulkheads create watertight compartments in the hull and make the ship rigid. A junk's sails, which are usually rectangular, are supported by many long strips of bamboo called battens. Smaller junks sail on China's rivers.

Navigation
Many navigation devices were invented by Arab astronomers and scientists. Measuring the height of the sun at noon with an astrolabe, helped sailors to work out their latitude.

A Chinese invention
The Chinese were the first people to use the compass. It appeared in China around 300 B.C., about 1,500 years before the West. The compass consisted of a magnetized iron needle floating in a bowl of water.

Zheng He's expeditions
In the early 1400s, Chinese navigator Zheng He went on several voyages of conquest and exploration along China's coast. He commanded a large fleet of junks—large vessels that dwarfed European ships of the time. However, in the 1430s, China adopted a policy of isolation and all exploration stopped.

Anchor

Bamboo batten

Rectangular sail made of thin cloth

Sails and battens
The bamboo battens that support a junk's sails have several advantages: they stiffen the sail, allow it to be taken down quickly, and provide a useful ladder for sailors to climb to the look out.

Crew's quarters

European caravel from the 1400s.

Pens for animals captured on voyages

Zheng He once brought a giraffe back from a voyage

Watertight bulkhead

Voyages of discovery

During the 1400s and 1500s, explorers set out from Spain and Portugal in search of the best route to Asia. They wanted to reach the Far East and bring back the rare, valuable spices that grew there, such as pepper, nutmeg, and cloves. A number of these explorers were employed by Prince Henry of Portugal, who became known as Henry the Navigator. They traveled in tiny ships, risking their lives on unknown waters, in the hope of making their fortunes. Those who succeeded discovered places, such as North America and parts of Africa, that were unknown to Europeans at the time.

Caravels
Many of the early Portuguese explorers favored small ships called caravels. These lightweight vessels had crews of about 25 people and were ideal in coastal waters. They had lateen (triangular) sails, which could take advantage of side winds.

Christopher Columbus
Christopher Columbus was born in Genoa, Italy, but his journeys were financed by the Spanish royal family. His four voyages to the West Indies opened up routes across the Atlantic Ocean.

First around the world
In 1519, Ferdinand Magellan set off from Portugal with five ships and 260 men. During the voyage, most of the crew—including Magellan—died and four ships were lost. But, in 1522, 18 men returned home, having traveled all the way around the world.

The New World
Columbus hoped to reach the East Indies by sailing westwards across the Atlantic Ocean, rather than following the eastward route of the Portuguese explorers. At this time, no one knew North America existed, so when Columbus discovered some new islands, he thought he had reached the East Indies. In fact, he had arrived in the Caribbean, and stumbled on a "new" world. On later voyages, he sailed along the coast of Central America, and visited Trinidad and many of the Caribbean islands.

Bowsprit

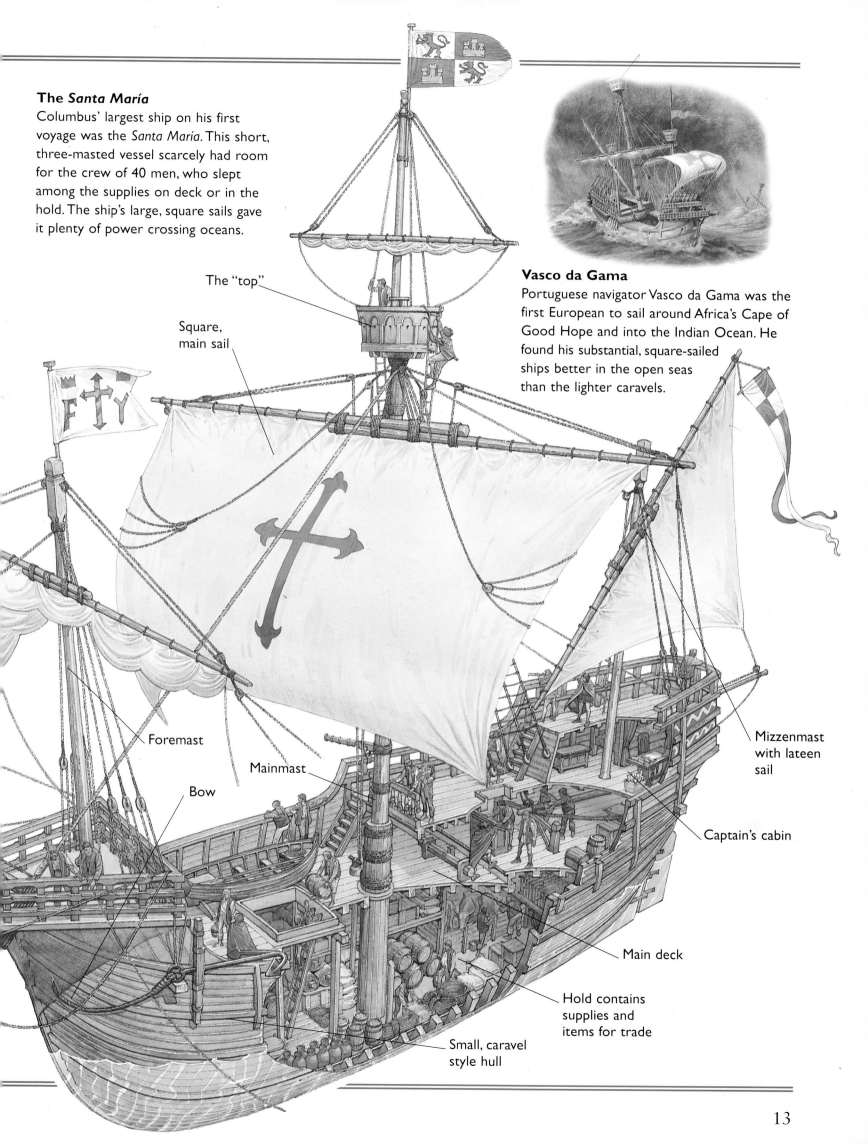

The *Santa María*

Columbus' largest ship on his first voyage was the *Santa María*. This short, three-masted vessel scarcely had room for the crew of 40 men, who slept among the supplies on deck or in the hold. The ship's large, square sails gave it plenty of power crossing oceans.

The "top"

Square, main sail

Vasco da Gama

Portuguese navigator Vasco da Gama was the first European to sail around Africa's Cape of Good Hope and into the Indian Ocean. He found his substantial, square-sailed ships better in the open seas than the lighter caravels.

Foremast

Mainmast

Bow

Mizzenmast with lateen sail

Captain's cabin

Main deck

Hold contains supplies and items for trade

Small, caravel style hull

Mapping the world

When the northern Europeans saw the riches that the Spanish and Portuguese were bringing back from the Far East, they, too, wanted a share of the wealth. The southern routes to Asia were long and dangerous, so countries such as England, France, and the Netherlands sent navigators to find shorter, northern routes. Some tried to find a way across North America (the "Northwest Passage") others went north of Russia (the "Northeast Passage"). The routes were too icy, but both led explorers into new waters, from Canada to Lapland.

Early mapping
Navigators recorded the coastlines and ports they visited so they could make maps. Gradually, more and more parts of the world were mapped, with Australia and the Americas the last land masses to be shown in detail.

Latitude
A cross-staff was an instrument that determined the latitude of a ship (distance from the equator). It worked by measuring the height of the North Star from the horizon.

The explorers of northern Europe

The search for new routes to the Far East sent British, French, and Dutch explorers deep into the icy waters of the north Atlantic Ocean and the Norwegian Sea. Their small ships were modeled after the carrack—a warship with a combination of lateen and square sails. Despite the skill of the sailors, many of the ships were lost in the rough northern seas. A sailor's life was usually filled with danger and tended to be short! The sailors that survived found no new route to the Far East, but they explored the little known waters of the north Atlantic, the lakes and rivers of Canada, and the seas around Greenland, Iceland, and Norway.

Navigation

The first explorers found their way by sailing along the coast, keeping land in view. When they sailed out to sea, they needed instruments to help locate their position. The most important instruments were the compass and a number of devices used to calculate latitude.

Willem Barents

Dutch explorer Willem Barents made several journeys in the 1590s in search of a Northeast Passage to the Indies. He sailed north up the coast of Norway, and explored the waters north of Lapland, which were later renamed the Barents Sea.

All around the world

British seaman Francis Drake sailed around the world in 1577–1580. Of his fleet of five ships, only the flagship, the 100-ton *Golden Hind*, completed the voyage.

Jacques Cartier (1491–1557)

This French explorer tried to find the Northwest Passage. He sailed up the St. Lawrence River to Hochelaga (now Montreal, Canada) and explored the waters around Newfoundland.

Compass

Invented in China, the magnetic compass appeared in Europe in c.1200. Sailors quickly started to use it to find their direction, even though early compasses were not always accurate.

Jolly Roger
The first pirate flags were red. It is thought that the French words *joli rouge* (pretty red) became the English term "Jolly Roger." Each pirate band had its own flag, which bore a variety of symbols such as a skeleton, skull and swords, or a skull and crossbones. Sailors quickly learned to recognize, and fear, all of them.

Piracy on the high seas

For as long as ships have sailed the seas, there have been pirates—people who rob and plunder ships for their cargo. Pirates always used fast ships—galleys with both sails and oars, four-masted galleons for raiding out at sea, or swift, sleek sloops with triangular sails for coastal waters. Pirates not only had to be frightening, they had to be skilled sailors, constantly adjusting the ships' rigging to get the best speed.

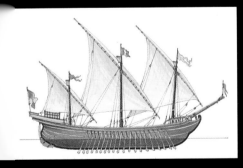

Barbary corsairs
Muslim pirates from the North African (or "Barbary") coast were known as "Barbary corsairs." They traveled in slim, fast galleys powered by both sails and oars, enabling them to make sudden attacks and quick getaways.

Pieces-of-eight
Spanish adventurers took gold and silver from the Americas and made it into coins called doubloons and pieces-of-eight. Pirates prized these coins—one gold doubloon was worth almost two months of a sailor's pay.

Caribbean pirates

Piracy was common in the Caribbean Sea in the 1600s and 1700s. The pirates began as buccaneers, defending their islands from marauding Spanish ships. But they later took to the seas as robbers, attacking any ship that promised plenty of riches.

Blackbeard

The most famous of the Caribbean pirates was Blackbeard. He struck terror into his victims with his cruelty. When the British navy finally caught and killed him, they hung his head from the bowsprit of their ship.

The pirate and his plunder

Pirates sailed under any flag they could lay their hands on. Unrecognized by their victims, they would come close to a ship before hoisting the Jolly Roger in the hope of scaring the crew into surrendering. Then they would board and take their treasures, killing anyone who got in their way. Favorite targets in the 1600s were Spanish ships returning from the Americas loaded with treasure. East Indiamen (trade ships that traveled from the Far East to Europe), and merchant vessels in the Mediterranean and China Seas were also popular prizes.

Modern pirates

In spite of the efforts of coastguards, pirates are still active in some parts of the world. Piracy often increases at times of political unrest and war.

Science on the seas

Line of latitude

Line of longitude

Longitude
The lines of longitude are great circles around the earth, crossing at the North and South Poles.

The 1700s were an age of great advances in science. The first explorer to be interested in scientific discovery was James Cook, a British sea captain. Cook went on three voyages to the Pacific, making astronomical observations, documenting wildlife, and plotting charts as he traveled. He was the first European to sail along the east coast of Australia.

Calculating longitude

Sailors had many difficulties working out their exact position at sea. They could establish their latitude by looking at the position of the sun, but the best way to calculate longitude required knowing the time difference between where you are and the time at home (one hour equals 15° longitude). But early clocks were not very accurate. English clockmaker John Harrison set out to make a special clock, called a chronometer, that could be used at sea.

The *Endeavour*
Cook sailed on the *Endeavour* on his first three Pacific voyages. The ship was originally designed to carry coal, so Cook knew it would be sturdy and able to carry a heavy load.

Harrison's chronometer
Finished in 1760, Harrison's fourth chronometer was the size of a large pocket watch. A copy of it was tested at sea by Captain Cook and it proved to be extremely accurate. Harrison was eventually awarded a large sum of money for solving the longitude problem.

Scientific work

Cook took with him on his travels an astronomer and two botanists, along with artists who drew all the plants and animals they saw. These included many species unknown outside the Pacific.

British "limeys"

One of Cook's more unusual discoveries was of a medical nature. Sailors on long voyages suffered from scurvy, a disease that causes puffy, painful gums and bleeding below the skin. Cook realized that scurvy could be prevented if the sailors ate plenty of fruits and vegetables. He gave his men sauerkraut and citrus fruit including limes and lemons, and the sailors did not develop the disease. Eventually, all British sailors adopted a similar diet, which is why they were nicknamed "limeys." We now know that it is the vitamin C in these foods that prevents scurvy.

Limes

Captain Cook

James Cook went to sea as a boy, and rose through the ranks of the navy, earning his first command at the age of 31. He did important survey work along the coasts of North America before his Pacific journeys. Cook tried to stay on good terms with the people he met on his journeys, but was killed in a fight with islanders in Hawaii in 1779.

The *Beagle*

In 1832, British scientist Charles Darwin joined the *Beagle* as the ship's naturalist on a voyage to South America. The ten-gun brig was rebuilt for the journey, but was still small. Darwin packed his quarters with the specimens he collected—material he would use in his groundbreaking book, *The Origin of Species*.

Ships for science

After the pioneering voyages of Captain Cook, many scientists were drawn to the sea. Individuals like Charles Darwin collected specimens that provided evidence for major scientific theories. But scientists realized that they knew little about the sea itself. In 1872, this began to change. The *Challenger*, the first ship designed for ocean research, sailed around the world, collecting data about the oceans and their wildlife. The science of oceanography was born.

The *Fram*

In the 1800s, Norwegian scientist and explorer Fridtjof Nansen had the *Fram* specially designed for Arctic exploration. The *Fram*'s hull was strengthened so that if the ice pressed against the ship's sides, it would not be crushed by the pressure.

Deep-sea explorer
Modern underwater explorers
need a research ship fitted with
laboratories, accommodations for
a team of scientists, space for all their
supplies, and a vessel that can dive
deep beneath the ocean's surface.
Oceanographic vessels, therefore,
can be large, although the
actual explorer craft needs
to be small and easily
maneuverable.

Research ship

Alvin

The *Alvin*
The deep-sea vessel
Alvin can carry people to
13,120 ft. (4,000m) below
sea level. It is easy to maneuver,
enabling explorers to discover
previously unknown creatures
hiding among the rocks.

The *Trieste*
The *Trieste* was one of the first bathyscaphes.
The heavily reinforced hull was designed to
withstand the tremendous water pressure
at the bottom of the sea. *Trieste* was the
first vessel to explore the Marianas Trench,
the deepest part of the Pacific Ocean.

Mysteries of the deep
People have always been
fascinated by the depths of
the sea. But until the 1900s,
the high water pressure, the
dark, and the cold stopped
people from deep-sea
exploration. In 1934, inventor
Charles William Beebe built the
bathysphere, a hollow, steel ball large
enough for a person, which is lowered on a chain
from a ship. In it Beebe explored the Atlantic Ocean
to depths of 2,952 ft. (900m). Stronger submersibles,
like the bathyscaphes (deep boats) and specially built
submarines with strengthened hulls, such as the
Alvin, were needed to explore even deeper.

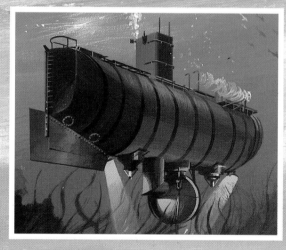

Clipper ships

With their long, slim hulls and large, billowing sails, the clippers of the 1800s were among the most elegant ships. Their huge, numerous sails meant that they were fast in a good wind, but could also keep moving in calm conditions. The first clippers were built in the United States. They were compact ships, but worked in areas where speed was more important than size, carrying valuable cargo across the oceans, for example. The most important cargo was tea, which they carried from China, across the Indian and Atlantic oceans, to Europe.

Sailors at work

Clippers needed a large crew to adjust the sails as the wind changed. Often, this could be done from deck, but sometimes sailors had to climb up the rigging, clinging to soaking, slippery sails to secure the canvas to the yard (beam).

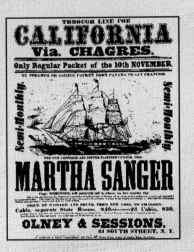

Recreation

Sailors filled the time between sleep and work with craft activities. The art of carving whalebone, shells, or ivory, called scrimshaw, was popular. Other sailors made model ships or worked on their knots, hitches, and splices.

Gold rush

In 1848, gold was discovered in California. Many people rushed to the west coast of the United States on board clippers to seek their fortunes. Sailors frequently jumped ship in California, so clippers had to take on extra crew for the rest of the trip to China.

In the harbor
This photograph from the late 1800s shows both clippers and steamships unloading their cargo at New York's South Street Seaport. By this time, most clippers had lightweight iron hulls, allowing them to carry heavier cargo.

New ships, new cargo
Clippers ruled the seas for 20 years before steamships took over their trade. In 1869, the Suez Canal opened, giving the big steamers an advantage over the small clippers. It enabled ships to pass directly through Egypt from the Mediterranean Sea to the Gulf of Suez instead of sailing all around Africa, shortening the journey by 6,000 miles (9,700km) and making speed less of an advantage. But larger clippers—four times the size of the first clippers—bringing bulkier cargo like wool and grain from Australia to England still had an important role.

Racing across the seas
Built for speed, clipper ships like the *Sir Lancelot* took 85 to 90 days to sail from Melbourne, Australia, to London, England, making them the swiftest vessels of their day.

World trade today

The world's largest ships are cargo carriers, with the largest of these being oil tankers. These tremendous ships can weigh as much as 500,000 tons when fully loaded. Because of computerized control and navigation systems, they are also able to sail with a small crew. Other types of cargo are carried by ships built to hold metal containers. With their huge hulls and decks, many modern container ships have room for more than 6,000 containers.

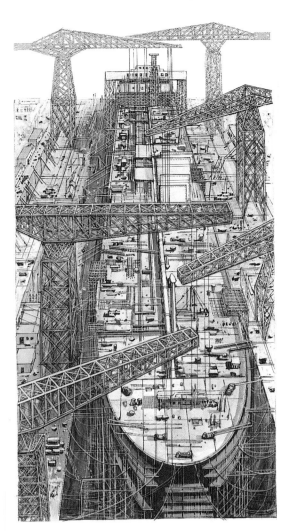

Shipbuilding
Building a modern cargo ship is a huge project needing a large workforce and major financial investment. Only a few of the world's shipyards have facilities big enough to build these monsters of the seas. Japan is the world's leading shipbuilding country.

Containers
The containers loaded on container ships come in two standard sizes, one exactly twice the size of the other.

In port
Modern cargo ships are built to hold large numbers of containers. These metal boxes are built to a standard size so that they can be stacked together safely. In port, a specially designed crane removes the containers one by one, and loads them onto waiting trains or trucks. A large modern port, such as Singapore, or Rotterdam in the Netherlands, may have many docking places—or quays—and cranes, so that dozens of ships can be loaded and unloaded at the same time.

Pollution

When an oil tanker is involved in an accident, oil can spread for miles in a thin "slick" on the surface of the sea. Damage to wildlife and beaches can take years to repair.

Trade on the seas

Modern container ships are ideal for transporting considerable quantities of heavy cargo around the world. The world's large ports are built to be "container friendly." They have docks and cranes large enough for the long-haul container ships, and are at key points on the main long-distance trade routes. Containers may be unloaded from long-haul vessels onto smaller, "feeder" ships for a shorter sea journey before finally being transferred to trains or trucks.

On the bridge

The captain has a good view of the sea and is aided by the latest navigational instruments. Captains still need the services of pilots—a sailor with local knowledge—to help guide the vessel safely into port.

On shore

Trucks and railroad cars are built to standard sizes so that they can take containers from any docked ship.

SHIPS OF WAR

From the earliest times, people have used ships in war. While early navies used their ships as troop carriers, or as giant battering rams, modern warships carry sophisticated weapons designed to fight enemies, either on sea or in the air, from a great distance.

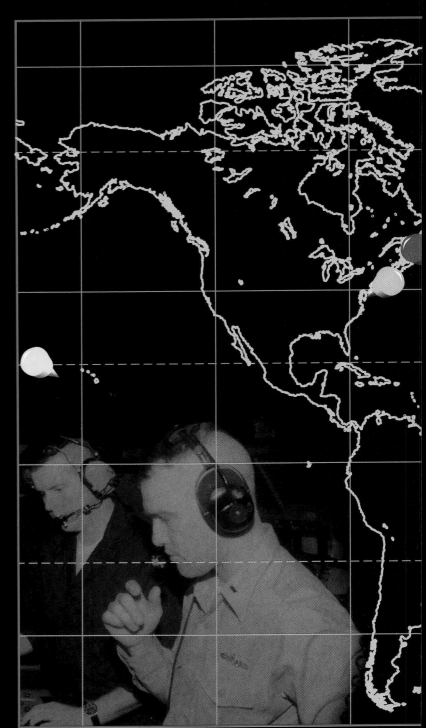

 Salamis 480 B.C.
Triremes, oar-powered warships from Greece, defeated a much larger fleet from Persia in this major battle, which stopped the Persians invading Greece.

 Aegospotami 405 B.C.
In a surprise attack off Thrace (northwest Turkey), the Spartans defeated Athens, capturing 170 Athenian ships during the Peloponnesian war.

Lepanto 1571
In the last great galley battle, the powerful Turkish navy was crushed by a large fleet formed by an alliance of Rome, Venice, and Spain.

Spanish Armada
In 1588, Philip II of Spain sent his fleet of sailing ships to try to invade England. They were defeated by the English navy and the stormy weather.

 Battle of Trafalgar
In 1805, British men-of-war, led by Admiral Nelson, defeated French and Spainish ships, foiling French emperor Napoleon's plans to invade England.

 Constitution vs Guerrière 1812–14
The *Constitution* earned its nickname *Old Ironsides* in a battle during the War of 1812 when it defeated the British ship *Guerrière*.

Monitor vs Merrimack 1862
The Civil War saw the first battle between ironclad warships. War at sea would never be the same again after this struggle.

Tsushima 1905
In a decisive battle of the war between Russia and Japan, Japanese cruisers and destroyers sunk 12 of their opponent's ships and captured four more.

Jutland 1916
The fleets of Germany and Britain clashed in this key battle of World War I. Both sides lost many ships; as a result the Germans turned to submarine warfare.

Midway 1942
In this turning point on the Pacific front of World War II, the United States navy sank four Japanese aircraft carriers, but lost only one carrier of its own.

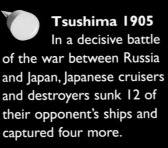

Galleys
The swiftest of their time, these oar--powered ships of ancient Greece and Rome had huge rams on the front to pierce the hulls of enemy ships.

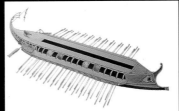

Early battleships
Warships like English King Henry VIII's *Mary Rose* carried guns and were also designed to get close to enemy ships so the crew could board them.

Men-of-war
In the 1700s, warships carried many large sails. They had rows of guns on several decks, which could be fired together in a broadside attack.

Ironclads
Iron warships first appeared in North America in the 1800s. They were powered by steam engines, so navies no longer had to rely on the wind.

Dreadnought
Fast, maneuverable and well-armed, British dread-noughts changed the face of warships at the start of the 1900s. Soon other nations were building similar ships.

Aircraft carriers
These large, floating runways can take military aircraft near the battlefield. These huge, expensive fighting ships can play a decisive role in a war.

Early warships

The ancient Greeks and Romans sailed into battle on galleys—long ships that carried both sails and oars. The oars were important because they gave the ship extra power, regardless of the wind. This provided good speed and the ability to attack an enemy vessel, using the great ram on the prow to make a hole in its side. The Greeks and Phoenicians developed biremes, with two rows of oars on each side, which gave them plenty of power despite their lightweight hulls.

The Phoenicians
A seafaring people from the eastern Mediterranean, the Phoenicians sailed biremes. These ships had a large ram, and a single mast with a square sail.

Triremes
The Greeks wanted to make bigger, more powerful ships. But if they added extra oarsmen, the ship would have had a longer hull, and this would have reduced its speed. They developed the trireme, a ship with three banks of oars staggered one above the other so that they took up less space.

Pulling together
Early Greek warships were small, with fewer than 30 oars on each side. Everyone had to pull at exactly the right time, so a huge drum was used to beat out a clear rhythm for the rowers.

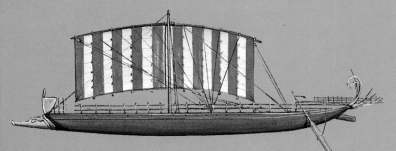

Roman warships
The Romans copied Greek designs for their warships, but built them using heavier timber, and sometimes added an extra mast. The Romans also improved the design of boarding bridges. A Roman boarding bridge had strong hinges and a spike that pinned the bridge to the deck of an enemy ship.

Into battle

The captain of a trireme would first try to "hole" an enemy ship by ramming it. As the oarsmen rowed and the ship gathered speed, the great ram crashed through the enemy's timbers. Then a wooden boarding bridge was thrown over the gap between the vessels, soldiers dashed across, and hand-to-hand fighting began.

Prow rams enemy ship

Boarding bridge

The Normans

For hundreds of years warship technology changed very little. In the 1000s, the Normans had ships similar to those used by the Scandinavian Vikings. Their ships had large, square sails set on masts that were lowered on landing. A side rudder was used for steering, and the vessel could be rowed in calm weather.

A naval invasion

The Bayeux Tapestry depicts the 1066 Norman invasion of England, from the crossing of the English Channel to the decisive Battle of Hastings. It also shows what Norman warships looked like.

Built for war

During the years A.D. 1000 to A.D. 1500, many warships, like the small, broad-beamed cogs, were simply converted cargo vessels. But soon ships were being built especially for war. These fighting machines were still small, but they had more sails, which gave them greater speed and maneuverability. They also had "castles" fore and aft, and "fighting tops" on the masts where archers could stand. In later years, they carried cannons to destroy enemy ships.

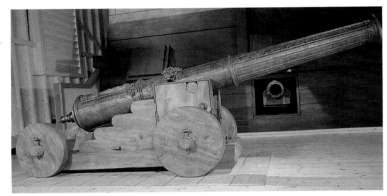

Cannon fire
The warship *Mary Rose* carried many large cannons made of bronze or wrought iron. Each front-loading gun was mounted on its own wheeled carriage, so that it could be rolled back for cleaning and reloading.

The *Mary Rose*
One of King Henry VIII of England's favorite ships, the *Mary Rose*, sank off the south coast of England in 1545. Archaeologists found the wreck and brought it to the surface, revealing a lot about the warships of the 1500s. The *Mary Rose* was built of carvel planking—instead of overlapping, the planks are laid edge to edge—on a framework of oak. The ship's four masts bore square sails.

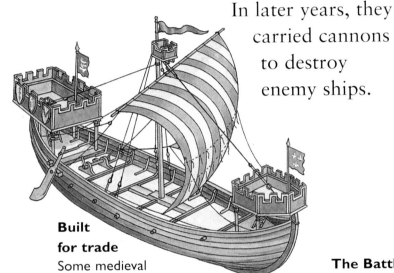

Built for trade
Some medieval merchant ships looked a lot like Viking ships, with square sails and side rudders, but with castles fore and aft. Later, ships were steered with stern rudders.

The Battle of Lepanto
In 1571, at Lepanto in the Mediterranean, the Turkish fleet fought with ships from Spain, Venice, Genoa, and the Papal States in the last battle involving oar-powered galleys. Well-armed, high-sided Venetian ships played an important part in the defeat of the Turkish forces.

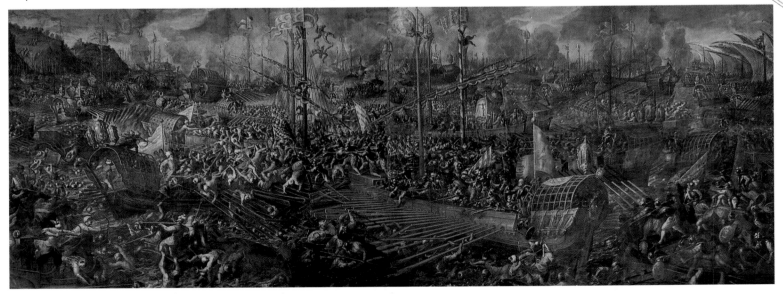

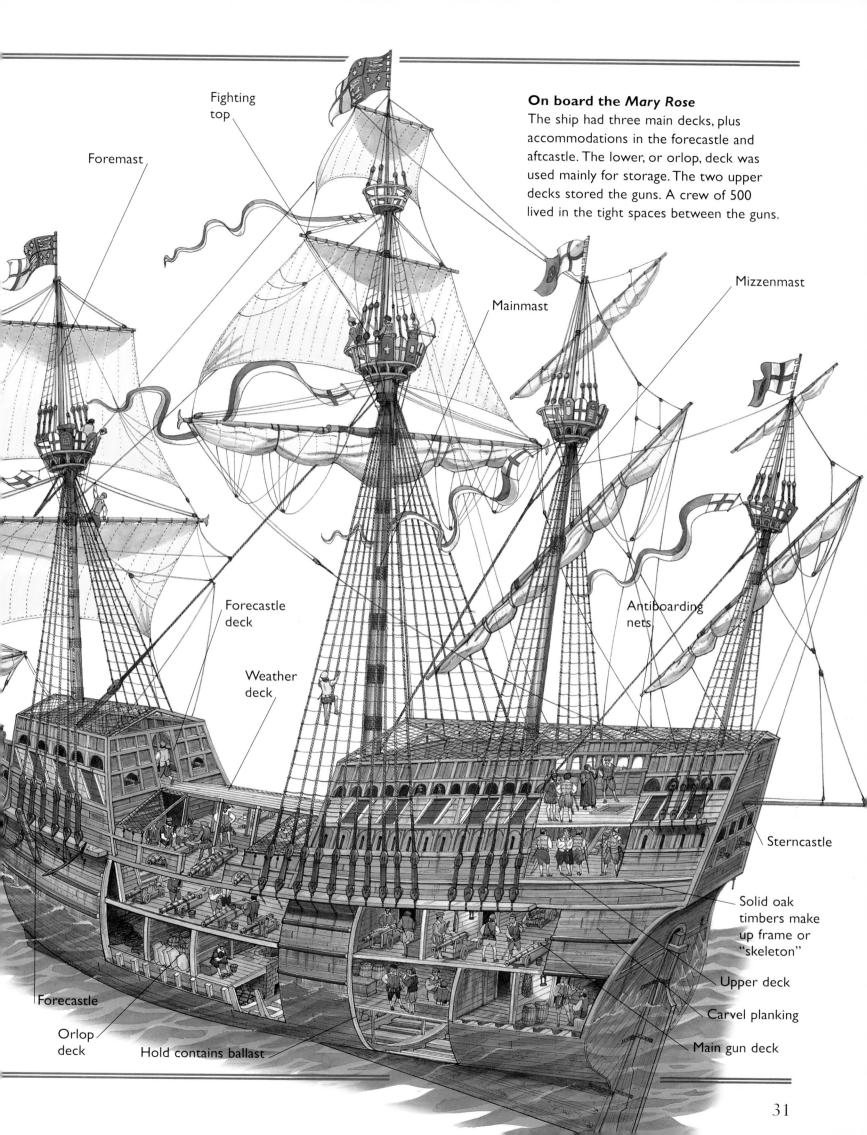

Fighting top

Foremast

On board the *Mary Rose*
The ship had three main decks, plus accommodations in the forecastle and aftcastle. The lower, or orlop, deck was used mainly for storage. The two upper decks stored the guns. A crew of 500 lived in the tight spaces between the guns.

Mainmast

Mizzenmast

Forecastle deck

Weather deck

Antiboarding nets

Sterncastle

Solid oak timbers make up frame or "skeleton"

Upper deck

Forecastle

Carvel planking

Orlop deck

Hold contains ballast

Main gun deck

31

Galleons

These large wooden fighting ships appeared on the seas during the 1400s. They were slender with beaklike prows, and their sides sloped inward, making them very stable. This was important because they carried rows of large, heavy cannons. Galleons were complex and costly to build—up to 2,000 oak trees were needed for each ship. But they were worth it. Galleons ruled the oceans for over 300 years. Some were even used for trade, bringing gold and silver from the Americas to Europe.

An English galleon

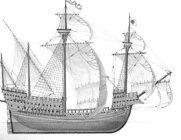

A Spanish galleon

Spanish Armada

Hoping to invade England in 1588, the king of Spain sent a fleet, or armada, of 151 ships. The English navy defended themselves with more than 200 galleons that were smaller and faster than those of the Spanish. The fighting lasted for ten days, with the English using cannons and sending fire ships—ships carrying explosives—to damage the armada. Finally, threatened by difficult winds and shallow waters, the Spanish withdrew.

Battling the Armada

The Spanish were used to battles in which they boarded their enemies' ships and fought hand-to-hand. But the English kept them at a distance, preventing them from boarding. The English also made full use of their galleons' cannons—which had a longer range than the Spanish guns—to damage their opponents' ships.

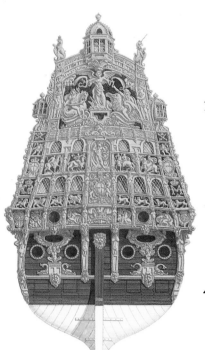

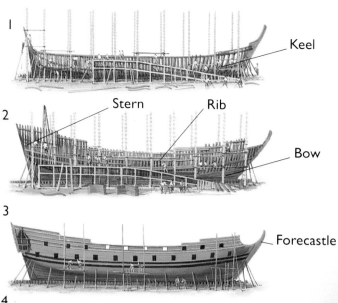

Keel

Stern   Rib

Bow

Forecastle

Hull

Building a galleon

Using the keel as the ship's "backbone" (1), shipbuilders added the ribs
and formed the bow and stern (2). The hull was covered with planks and
the decks built as construction went along (3). Next the forecastle took
shape—it did not overhang like those on earlier ships, making the galleon
more stable. Finally, the hull was waterproofed with tar (4).

The Anglo-Dutch wars

During the 1600s, the English and the Dutch
went to war three times over sea trade and fishing
rights. The English fleet was made up of galleons
that were better armed than the Dutch ships. In
the first Anglo-Dutch war (1652–54), the English
took advantage of their strength to gain decisive
victories. The Dutch responded in the second war
(1665–67) by destroying the English fleet while
it was docked. The third conflict (1672–74)
was more evenly matched.

Galleons at war

Here, an English galleon makes a
broadside attack on a Dutch ship,
bringing down its masts and sending
the crew overboard. The Dutch fire
back, but only managed to damage
their opponents' sails.

Men-of-war

The great wooden warships of the 1700s and 1800s were called "men-of-war." They carried crews of up to 800 sailors on long, perilous journeys into battle. The crews had to put up with damp, cramped, and dangerous conditions. They also had to be highly skilled—climbing the masts and rigging to unfurl the huge sails on the three main masts in a matter of minutes.

Rear view
This view of the French ship *Soleil Royal* shows the stern. It contained the officers' quarters. Ship sterns were rarely attacked, so they were often ornate and had many windows.

The press-gang
Few people wanted to join the navy, so ships sent out groups of men, called press-gangs, to get new recruits. If they could not persuade anyone to join, they took men by force.

Life on board
Life was hard on board a man-of-war. The food, ranging from salt meat to dried peas and hard biscuits, was poor quality and usually rotten. Ordinary sailors had no privacy—they had to do everything from sleeping to going to the bathroom in full view of everyone. But there was always plenty to do—mending and rigging the sails, scrubbing the deck, and repairing the ship's planks.

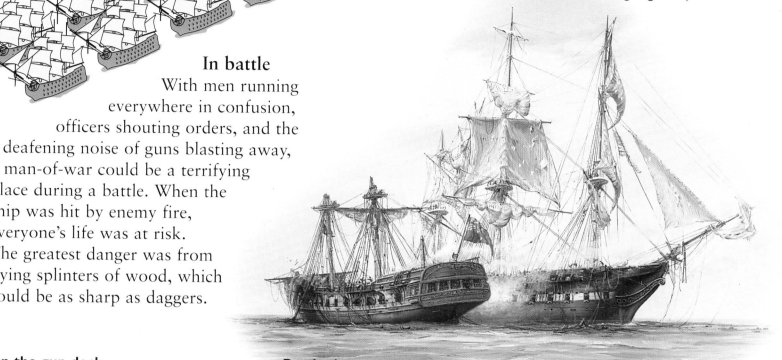

Battle formation

Enemy fleets drew together slowly at the start of a battle. Their guns were accurate only at short range, so they waited until they were close to the enemy ship before attacking broadside (all the guns on one side firing together).

In battle

With men running everywhere in confusion, officers shouting orders, and the deafening noise of guns blasting away, a man-of-war could be a terrifying place during a battle. When the ship was hit by enemy fire, everyone's life was at risk. The greatest danger was from flying splinters of wood, which could be as sharp as daggers.

On the gun deck

As men loaded the guns and got ready to fire, young boys called "powder monkeys" ran across the deck with gunpowder from the magazine (storeroom). Then everyone stood clear, because the guns recoiled (jumped backward) as they fired.

Battle damage

In this painting, the American ship Constitution has defeated the British ship Guerrière in the War of 1812. Ship carpenters could repair damage to a hull, but could do little about the masts and rigging. Without working sails, a ship was disabled, and the enemy crew could board her.

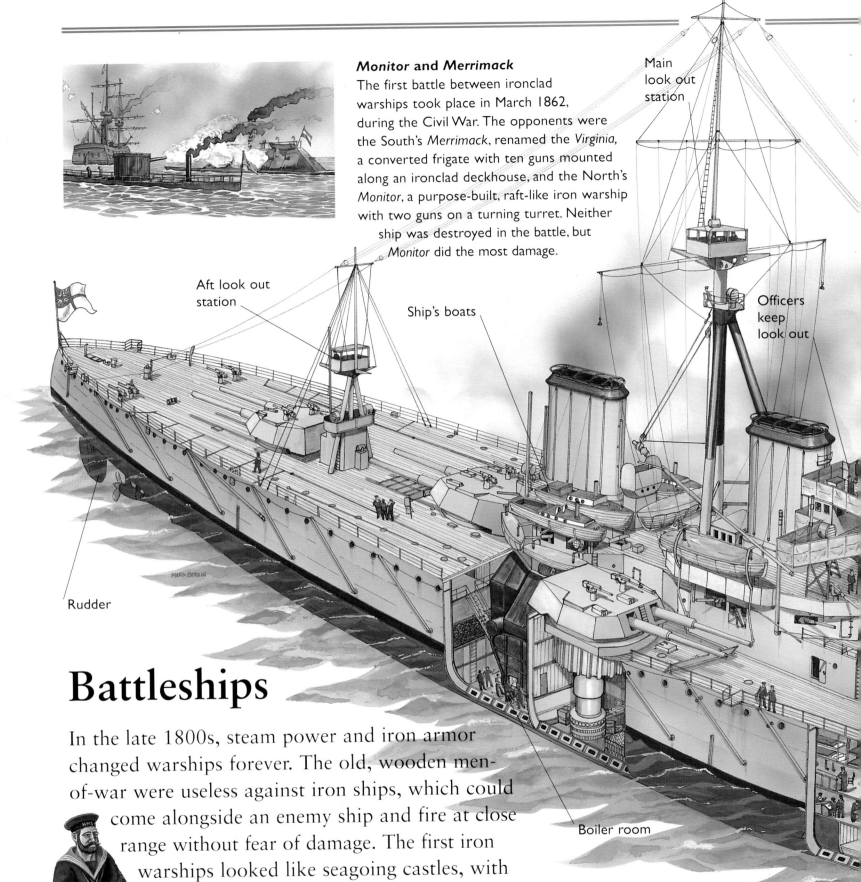

Monitor and Merrimack
The first battle between ironclad warships took place in March 1862, during the Civil War. The opponents were the South's *Merrimack*, renamed the *Virginia*, a converted frigate with ten guns mounted along an ironclad deckhouse, and the North's *Monitor*, a purpose-built, raft-like iron warship with two guns on a turning turret. Neither ship was destroyed in the battle, but *Monitor* did the most damage.

Main look out station

Aft look out station

Ship's boats

Officers keep look out

Rudder

Boiler room

Battleships

In the late 1800s, steam power and iron armor changed warships forever. The old, wooden men-of-war were useless against iron ships, which could come alongside an enemy ship and fire at close range without fear of damage. The first iron warships looked like seagoing castles, with armored sides and tall gun turrets. Soon, shipbuilders were constructing huge battleships, such as the *Dreadnought*, which relied on a number of big guns fired together to damage or sink the enemy.

Below decks
Large parts of the hull of the *Dreadnought* were filled with ammunition for the ship's big guns and torpedo tubes. There were also fuel stores for its turbine engines. The engines themselves took up much less space than ordinary steam engines of similar power.

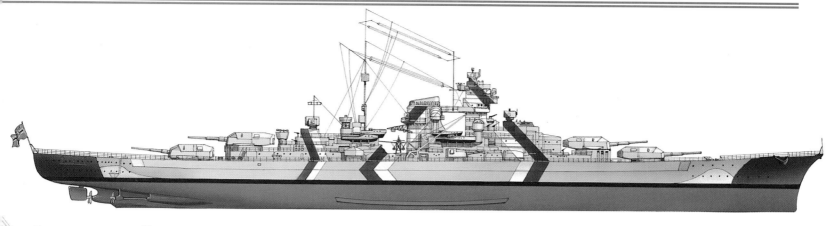

Large or small

In the 1900s, battleships got bigger and more powerful, with faster engines and larger guns. The world's navies competed with each other to build the biggest, most impressive battleships. During World War II, the Japanese developed the Yamato class of ship. Each Yamato warship weighed an amazing 74,168 tons, making them the largest battleships ever built. But few navies could afford such monster ships. After the war, they relied on long-range missiles fired from smaller and cheaper vessels.

The *Bismarck*

At 52,832 tons, the *Bismarck* was one of the largest German ships of World War II. It had a top speed of 35 mph. (56km/h) and large, 15 inch (38cm) bore guns. However, this awesome ship had a short career. It was sunk by the British navy in 1941, only two years after its launch.

The *Kirov*

In the 1970s and 1980s, the Soviet Union (Russia) built several *Kirov*-class nuclear battleships. Each of these large ships was powered by two on-board nuclear reactors. They were highly valued because they could sail for vast distances without refuelling. The vessels were scrapped in the 1990s because they were too expensive to service.

Gun turret

Officers' mess

Hold contains ammunition

Dreadnought

The British ship *Dreadnought* was launched in 1906. It had ten big guns, five torpedo tubes, but no small guns at all. It was also the first battleship to be driven by steam turbines, giving a top speed of 24 mph. (39km/h). This combination of speed and incredible fire power impressed naval commanders. Soon there were many imitations, and all large warships in the early 1900s became known as "dreadnoughts."

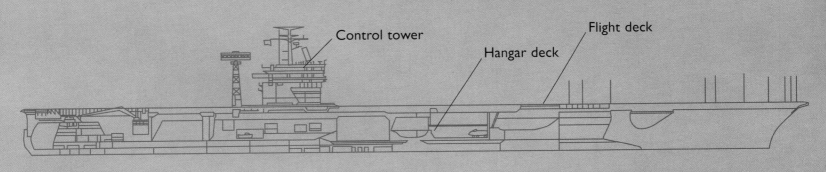

Control tower

Flight deck

Hangar deck

Battle fleet

Modern navies go into battle from a long distance. Their ships can fire guided missiles that travel hundreds of miles to their targets. They can also use aircraft carriers to deliver fighters and other airplanes to the war zone. A modern battle fleet may consist of either a large aircraft carrier defended by smaller ships called destroyers, or a number of smaller ships firing long-range missiles.

Inside the aircraft carrier

Much of the space below deck on the USS *Nimitz* aircraft carrier is taken up by accommodations for about 3,000 personnel. Two pressurized, water-cooled nuclear reactors power the *Nimitz* to speeds of over 34 mph. (56km/h) or 30 knots— impressive for a vessel the height of a 25-story building. Over 90 aircraft can be stored on the hangar deck.

USS *Enterprise*

The first nuclear-powered aircraft carrier, and the longest warship ever built, is the USS *Enterprise*. About 75 aircraft can take off from the 140,000 ft. (372m) long flight deck. The warship was launched in 1961, and is still in active service.

Missile destroyer

Traditionally destroyers were small, fast-moving warships, armed with both guns and torpedoes, and used for defending the main fleet and attacking submarines. Modern destroyers have guided missiles and perform a wide range of duties.

Aircraft carriers

The most impressive modern warships are aircraft carriers, enormous vessels with huge flight decks from which aircraft can take off and land. The ships are so large and expensive that only major powers, such as the United States, can afford them. They have played a key role in most modern conflicts, from World War II to the Gulf War and the Balkan conflict.

An aircraft waits to take off from the flight deck of the USS *John F. Kennedy*

The flight deck

Bomber and fighter planes, surveillance aircraft, anti-submarine planes, and helicopters can take off from the flight deck of a modern aircraft carrier. The deck has enough space for these aircraft to park, as well as a runway for take off and landing. Today warships use missiles, which have a longer range and greater accuracy than guns, to attack the enemy. Different types of missiles can be aimed at enemy ships or aircraft. Hi-tech equipment in the control tower allows everything to be controlled and monitored from a distance.

Viking settlers

During the 800s and 900s, the Vikings traveled far from their native Scandinavia. They founded settlements in Iceland and Greenland and, in 1001, reached the coast of Newfoundland. They were probably the first Europeans to reach North America.

California gold rush

When gold was discovered in California in 1848, people rushed there, hoping to make their fortunes. Land travel across North America was hard, so many traveled around South America to California by clipper ship.

NORTH AMERICA

Migration in the 1800s

Millions of people left Europe in the 1800s, to seek a better life in countries like the United States and Canada.

The Pilgrims

Braving long, hard journeys in tiny, poorly equipped ships, settlers like the Pilgrims peopled the east coast of North America in the 1600s.

SOUTH AMERICA

PEOPLING THE WORLD

Throughout history, people have left their homelands to start a new life in a new country. Ships, whether steamships from the 1800s or modern liners, have plenty of room for people and their luggage, so they have played a major role in these migrations.

Luxury liners

In the early 1900s, people traveled on huge passenger liners. The rich had luxury cabins and the poor had more basic accommodations.

Aircraft travel
In the 1950s and 1960s, jet aircraft became widespread and air fares started to fall. Many people took advantage of this faster means of transportation. The great age of sea travel was over.

EUROPE

ASIA

Refugees
When the Vietnam War ended in 1976, refugees fled the country, fearing the Communist government. Many escaped on boats, risking death by living on cramped, unseaworthy vessels.

Slave trade
Some European merchants became rich taking Africans on cramped ships to the United States as slaves. Many peole died in the appalling conditions on board the ships.

AFRICA

Steamships
In the 1800s, ships with steam engines became more reliable than sailing ships, and they were soon used for both long and short routes. Steamships were ideal wherever a regular service was needed.

COME TO AUSTRALIA

Migration to Australia
With a widespread publicity campaign, the government of Australia encouraged many people to settle in their country during the 1950s. Passenger liners offered cheap fares.

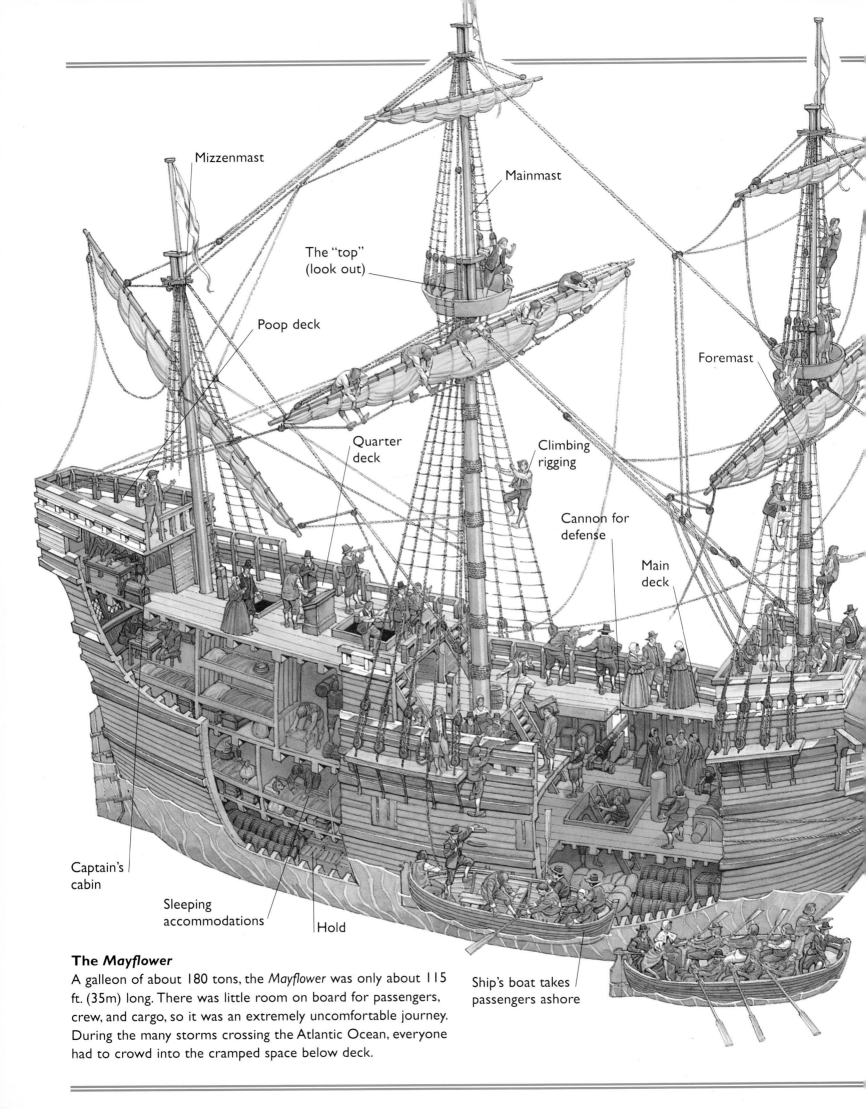

Mizzenmast

Mainmast

The "top" (look out)

Poop deck

Foremast

Quarter deck

Climbing rigging

Cannon for defense

Main deck

Captain's cabin

Sleeping accommodations

Hold

Ship's boat takes passengers ashore

The *Mayflower*

A galleon of about 180 tons, the *Mayflower* was only about 115 ft. (35m) long. There was little room on board for passengers, crew, and cargo, so it was an extremely uncomfortable journey. During the many storms crossing the Atlantic Ocean, everyone had to crowd into the cramped space below deck.

Early settlers

At many different times in history, from the Viking period to the 1900s, people have sailed to new homes. Their reasons range from famine to fortune hunting. One of the most famous migrations took place in 1620, when a group of people left England to establish a settlement in North America. Many of them wanted to leave their homeland because they could not practice their religious beliefs freely in England. They called themselves Pilgrims.

Thanksgiving
The Pilgrims celebrated their first year in North America, and their first harvest, with a special meal. They invited members of the local Wampanoag tribe to the feast.

The Pilgrim settlers
The Pilgrims' ship, the *Mayflower*, was already old when she left Plymouth, England. But she was sturdy enough to withstand a battering from many gales during the 66-day journey across the Atlantic. She carried 102 passengers and a crew of more than 40. One passenger died during the journey, but two more were born so they landed with one more passenger than they started out with.

Spritsail

Bowsprit

The landing
After landing at what is now Plymouth, Mass., the Pilgrims spent weeks looking for a place to settle. They established Plymouth Colony along Cape Cod Bay, and began to build houses there on Christmas Day in 1620.

Beakhead— about 20 ft. (6m) long

Wooden planks laid over oak frames

The slave trade

Between the 1600s and 1800s, millions of Africans were forcibly transported across the oceans and sold as slaves. Three continents were involved in this shameful trade. Ships left Europe with trade goods that were sold on the African coast. The ruthless captains took on a cargo of Africans, sailed to the United States, and sold them as slaves to plantation owners and wealthy merchants, before returning to Europe loaded with sugar or other produce. Not only did slaves have to endure appalling conditions on the ships, but they were also taken from their homes forever.

Capturing slaves

People taken as slaves were rounded up in gangs and marched to the coast. Here they were kept in pens called barracoons until an America-bound ship was ready for loading. As they boarded the ships, the slaves were held in leg-irons, with their hands tied behind their backs.

Slave ships

Most slave ships were small vessels of a few hundred tons originally designed to carry cargo. The Africans who were forced to travel on these vessels were treated like cargo, packed together tightly on the ships' small decks.

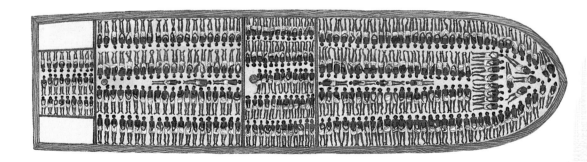

The sailors

Sailors on board a slave ship had little choice but to go along with the cruelty the slaves suffered. They, too, would have been punished if they showed any mercy. As well as maintaining discipline, they had to guard the slaves closely in case they tried to escape. Occasionally slaves tried to jump overboard, so captains often hung nets along the sides of the ships.

Life as a slave
Many slaves worked on plantations that grew cotton or tobacco in the southern United States, and on sugar plantations in the Caribbean. They had no legal rights, and were considered their owner's property.

Mealtime
Shipowners gave slaves little food on the journey. Most slaves arrived on the other side of the Atlantic Ocean thin, weak, and sick.

The journey
There was no space to move on a slave ship—people were crammed into every corner. The slaves also had to endure unsanitary conditions and a very poor diet. Disease spread quickly, and as many as 15 percent of the captives died during the journey. Others were maimed by the leg irons and metal collars they were forced to wear, or were injured by being forced to lie on the deck throughout the journey. All were terrified because they were leaving their homes to live in an unknown world.

From sail to steam

Until the 1800s, sea travel was slow and uncomfortable, discouraging people from traveling overseas. The Industrial Revolution brought about the introduction of steam-powered factories in Britain, and opened up the possibility of using steam engines at sea. This meant that ships would no longer have to rely on the wind to power their sails. Steamships allowed shipping companies to offer passengers a regular, reliable service. They were also used to transport cargo and carry overseas mail.

A great shipbuilder
The British engineer Isambard Kingdom Brunel worked on railroads and bridges before building his first steamship, the *Great Western*, in 1836–1837. This large, wooden paddle steamer was used for crossing the Atlantic Ocean. It was followed by the *Great Britain* and the huge *Great Eastern*, a 692-ft. (211m) steamer that could carry 4,000 passengers.

SS *Great Britain*
For his second steamship, the *Great Britain*, Brunel used screw propellers instead of paddle wheels. Propellers were more reliable than paddle wheels, which could be pushed out of the water in rough seas. He also built an iron hull, which was less prone to damage from the vibration of the gigantic engines.

Auxiliary sail

Iron rigging

Engine room

Promenade deck

Weather deck

Propeller

Steamships

The first experimental steamships appeared at the end of the 1700s. During the next 50 years a variety of steamships developed, from Brunel's large passenger vessels to small cargo ships designed for short journeys. Most of these ships also had sails— to save fuel when there were favorable winds, and as a source of power if the engines broke down.

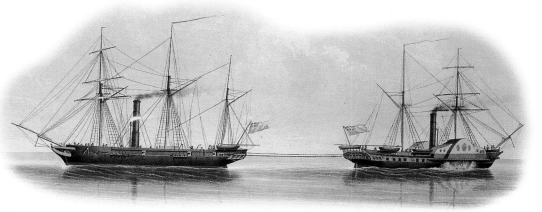

Trial of strength

People argued about whether paddle wheels or propellers were more powerful. In 1845, two similar British ships, the paddle steamer *Alecto* and the propeller-driven *Rattler*, took part in a tug-of-war. *Rattler* won the contest, pulling the paddle steamer backward at about 3 mph. (5km/h).

Mainmast

Foremast

38 ft. (11.5m) high funnel

Dining saloon

The *Sirius*

The first ship to cross the Atlantic Ocean using steam power, the *Sirius* was a small, 700-ton paddler. Brunel's *Great Western* began its crossing a few days after the *Sirius*, but arrived in the harbor in New York just a few hours after it. The *Great Western* had traveled at a higher average speed.

Passenger cabins

Forecastle

Emigration

During the 1800s, thousands of people left Europe, hoping for a better life in South Africa, Brazil, Canada, and the United States. They crossed the Atlantic Ocean on huge liners, and the great shipping companies, such as Cunard and the Red Star Line, competed for the business. Most of their travelers were poor and could afford only the cheapest accommodations on board. But they put up with the overcrowded conditions because they hoped they would lead a more prosperous life when they arrived in a new country.

Life on board

Most emigrants had never traveled on the ocean before, and the trip was a harrowing experience with cramped conditions and seasickness common. Once in port, the emigrants had to stay on board for days sometimes before being allowed to disembark. Then they had to pass through immigration control—they could be sent home if they did not have the right landing papers or were in poor health.

On board the ship

Even on luxury liners like the Cunard ship *Carpathia,* the cheapest accommodations, called steerage, were crowded and uncomfortable. Hundreds of emigrants were crammed into dark dormitories, getting what sleep they could on hard bunk beds.

CARPATHIA

Radio communication

Italian inventor Guglielmo Marconi pioneered radio communication. In 1901, he sent the first radio signals across the Atlantic Ocean. Radio communication made long sea journeys safer than before.

Points of departure

In the late 1800s, liners were getting bigger as well as faster. German shipowners were among the first to realize that with bigger ships they could make money out of the thousands of people who wanted to emigrate. Soon, ships from other northern European countries were also carrying large numbers of emigrants. Later, people from southern Europe began to make the journey.

ORIENT LINE
Via Suez Canal to
AUSTRALIA

To Australia

In the 1950s and 1960s, encouraged by the Australian government, which paid their fares, thousands of Europeans and Asians emigrated to Australia.

A new life

Full of hope, immigrants to the United States get their first glimpse of the Statue of Liberty in New York, welcoming them to the "land of the free."

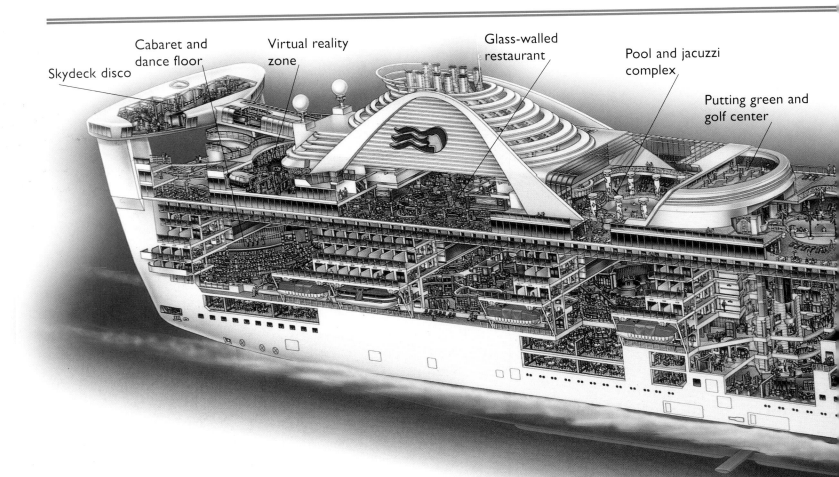

Skydeck disco

Cabaret and dance floor

Virtual reality zone

Glass-walled restaurant

Pool and jacuzzi complex

Putting green and golf center

Luxury travel

First class passengers on the liners of the early 1900s traveled in great style, a tradition continued today as many people enjoy cruises on luxurious ocean liners, traveling from country to country, and only going on shore to see the sights. Packed into a hull up to 984 feet (300m) in length, today's cruise ships contain cabins with every comfort—a range of places to eat and drink, a variety of entertainments, from movie theaters to casinos, and stores to swimming pools. Whether cruising the Mediterranean Sea or crossing the Atlantic Ocean, travelers are offered all the facilities they would expect on shore in a first-class hotel.

A life of ease
First class passengers on the liners of the early 1900s lived a life of great luxury, with all their needs attended to by a large crew.

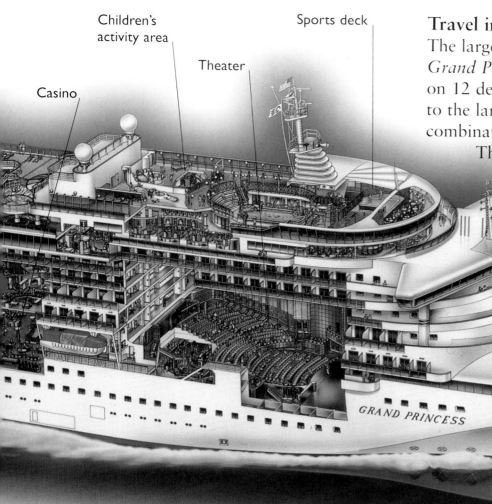

Casino

Children's
activity area

Theater

Sports deck

Travel in style

The largest cruise ship in the world, the *Grand Princess*, carries 2,600 passengers on 12 decks. From the staterooms and suites to the large public areas, the ship offers a combination of luxury and modern convenience. The facilities on board the *Grand Princess* include a library offering CD-ROM access, a virtual reality game area, a casino decorated with holograms, and a swimming pool with a retractable roof.

GRAND PRINCESS

The Blue Ribbon

Liners of the 1800s and early 1900s competed for the Blue Ribbon, an award for the fastest Atlantic Ocean crossing. The *Pacific*, won the award in 1851, averaging 15 mph. (24km/h). But this record was soon broken. The famous liner *Mauretania* held the Ribbon from 1907 until 1929 and reached a top speed of 31 mph. (50km/h).

Record breaker

One of the most successful liners of the 1930s, the *Normandie* was 977 ft. (298m) long and able to carry about 1,975 passengers and 1,345 crew. The hull was designed for speed, even in rough weather, and the *Normandie* crossed the Atlantic in under four days, earning the ship the Blue Ribbon.

NORMANDIE

DISCOVERING SHIPS

Over the centuries, ships have been used in a wide range of roles, and shipbuilding and navigation technologies have evolved dramatically. Historians and marine archaeologists research historical documents, paintings, myths, and folktales, as well as shipwrecks, to tell them about ships and life at sea in the past.

Titanic
This huge liner was said to be indestructible, but she was sunk by an iceberg in 1912 on her maiden voyage. Divers have found and studied the wreck, and salvaged objects from the ship.

Exxon Valdez
In 1989, the oil tanker *Exxon Valdez* ran aground off Alaska, spilling 13 million gallons (50 million liters) of oil and polluting thousands of miles of coastline.

Constitution
Some sailing ships, like the famous frigate *Constitution*, have been painstakingly restored by naval historians.

Spanish Armada
Many of the Spanish ships involved in Philip II's ill-fated attempt to invade Britain in 1588 were wrecked off the coast of Ireland.

Santa María
In 1492, Christopher Columbus sailed to North America on the *Santa María*, but the vessel was wrecked off the coast of the island of Hispaniola (modern Haiti).

NORTH AMERICA

SOUTH AMERICA

Medusa
Survivors of this famous 1800s shipwreck were painted by the French artist, Géricault.

The Vikings

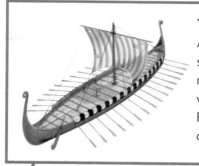

Although the Vikings were skilled sailors, they lost many ships in the stormy waters of the North Atlantic. Remains of their cargo are occasionally found.

Vasa

This Swedish royal warship from the 1600s was recovered from the seabed by marine archaeologists. The finely decorated timber hull is preserved in a museum.

Mary Rose

King Henry VIII's favorite battleship, the *Mary Rose*, sank in 1545. In 1982, marine archaeologists raised the ship.

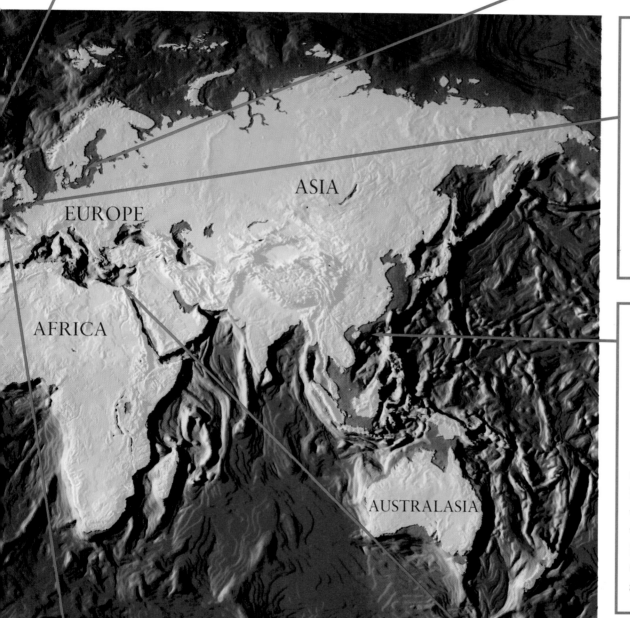

ASIA

EUROPE

AFRICA

AUSTRALASIA

Chinese junks

Many of these large vessels, their holds full with rich cargo, have been wrecked off the Chinese coast in the East and South China seas.

Bismarck

This large German battleship of World War II was sunk during an attack by British ships and aircraft in 1941, only two years after its launch.

Orient

The French flagship *Orient* exploded at the Battle of the Nile in 1798. Wreckage was widely scattered, but divers have found items such as cutlery and glassware intact.

Myths and mysteries

The sea has always been a frightening and hazardous place. No matter how skilled the captain and crew are, hidden rocks or punishing weather can bring a ship down. Throughout history, sailors have told stories about mythical creatures and mysterious forces, tales that try to explain some of the powers of the sea. Terrible monsters, gods of the winds, and beautiful—but deadly—mermaids are just a few of the mythical dangers lurking in the depths.

Odysseus and the sirens
In Greek legend, sirens were sea demons, half-woman and half-bird, whose beautiful song-lured sailors to their deaths on the rocks. The hero Odysseus survived hearing the song. He made his crew block their ears with wax and tie him to the mast.

Flying Dutchman
Germanic myths tell of the *Flying Dutchman*, whose captain sold his soul to the Devil in exchange for a safe passage around the Cape of Good Hope. But the captain made a fatal mistake. Because he did not ask to make the voyage only once, he was forced to sail back and forth forever.

Mary Celeste

The American cargo ship *Mary Celeste* left New York in November 1872, bound for Genoa, Italy. The following month she was found deserted, her sails set for stormy conditions and the ship's boat gone. The captain and crew were never seen again. They seemed to have abandoned ship in a hurry, but no one ever discovered what happened to them.

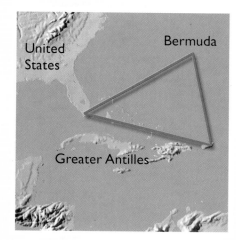

United States
Bermuda
Greater Antilles

Bermuda Triangle

Scientists are baffled by the mysterious disappearances of more than 50 ships in this part of the Atlantic Ocean, between Bermuda, the Great Antilles, and the southern coast of the United States.

Sailor's lore

Alone in the middle of a huge ocean, a ship can sail for days without sighting another vessel. If there is an accident, there is no one to explain how it happened. These mysteries have inspired sailors' tales of disappearing ships and vanishing crews. Stories about crafts dogged by misfortune and mishaps have led to many superstitions. Some sailors believe that it is unlucky to begin a voyage on Friday (the day of Jesus' crucifixion), others that the color green is unlucky, or that whistling when it is calm will bring on a storm. Having women and priests on board is also considered unlucky by some fishermen.

Viking prows

The wooden prows of Viking warships were carved with the heads of frightening mythical beasts—snarling dragons, hissing snakes, and terrifying bird-like creatures. They were probably intended to scare enemies and ward off evil spirits.

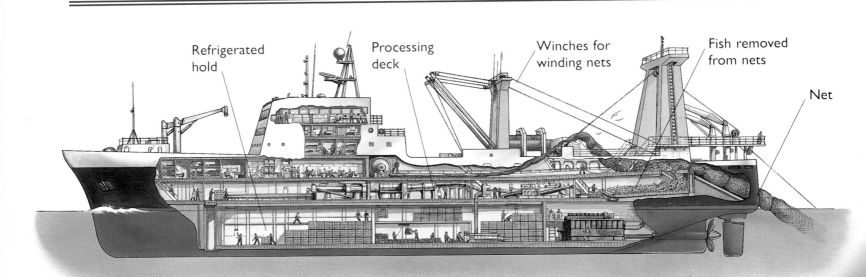

Refrigerated hold

Processing deck

Winches for winding nets

Fish removed from nets

Net

Other kinds of boats

There is a ship or a boat for virtually every job that needs to be done at sea. They range from gigantic oil tankers to oceangoing yachts, from flimsy row boats to lifeboats that go out in all weather to rescue those in trouble at sea. Although many of them look as if they have not changed for years, boats usually carry the most up-to-date technology, including powerful computers and satellite navigation.

Factory ship

With this type of ship, fish can be caught and processed while still at sea. As the nets are wound in, the fish are removed and conveyed to a processing deck, where they are scaled, cleaned, and filleted. Then they are packed into boxes, and frozen in the refrigerated hold.

Ferry crossings

Large ferry ships sail back and forth, carrying passengers and cars across many of the narrow channels of the world's seas. As well as several passenger decks, modern ferries also have car decks. When in dock, a section of the ship's bow opens to allow motor vehicles to drive on and off.

Catamarans

A catamaran is a boat with two hulls. Catamarans were developed in the Pacific islands thousands of years ago, but have only been used in the rest of the world for about 30 years. Having twin hulls makes the boat wide, so it is very stable and can carry large sails. The craft is also lightweight. This combination of features makes catamarans fast and ideal for racing.

Sport and recreation

Sailing is one of the world's most popular pastimes, and involves a variety of craft, from simple, fiberglass dinghies to luxury yachts fitted with every imaginable comfort. Sailing developed as a sport when sailing ships stopped being used for trade and battle. For racing, the aim is to build a boat that is lightweight, can carry big sails so it can go fast, and will handle well at sea. Racing boat designers often combine old and new materials, such as traditional woods and the latest hi-tech sail fabrics.

Salvage vessel

This Russian ship is a salvage tug that helps search for wreckage and survivors when ships have sunk or aircraft have gone down over the ocean. The ship carries a magnetic detector, to locate metal debris with ease.

Computer-controlled sails

Modern tankers, like this Japanese ship, sometimes have sails and engines. In this experimental vessel, an onboard computer sets the sails so that the ship can use wind power when the weather is favorable. The owners can sometimes save up to ten percent of the normal fuel costs this way.

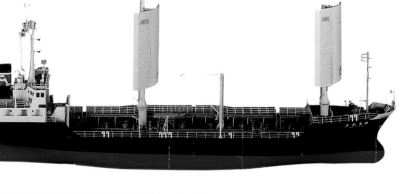

Shipwrecks

The sea is a dangerous place. Even experienced sailors respect its natural dangers—rocks, icebergs, unpredictable currents, unexpected storms—all of which can lead to a shipwreck. In times of war, ships are also in constant danger from enemy fire. The oceans and seabeds are littered with wrecks, from ancient Roman galleys to Spanish galleons and ocean liners. Their remains are fascinating—both for what they can tell about early ships, and for the treasure they sometimes contain.

The *Constitution*

The American ship *Constitution,* better known as *Old Ironsides,* was built in the 1790s. It was one of the fastest warships of its time. After taking part in the War of 1812, the *Constitution* had many jobs including carrying cargo and naval training. It was eventually restored to its original splendor and can be seen today at the Charlestown Navy Yard in Boston, Mass.

Wreck of the *Titanic*

On its maiden voyage in 1912, the *Titanic* hit an iceberg in the Atlantic Ocean. The ice ripped a hole in the ship's hull, and it sank to the bottom of the ocean, taking 1,490 lives with it.

The Vasa

The wooden hull of this Swedish ship, which sank on its maiden voyage in 1628, was discovered in 1956. The hull and thousands of artifacts were salvaged and preserved in a special museum. The Vasa gives a unique insight into life on a 1600s warship.

Finding the wreck

Salvage experts found the Titanic in 1985. Their cameras showed that the ship had broken into two sections, and the hull was hardly damaged. The salvage crew used a submersible and remote cameras to survey the wreck, and to bring fittings and other items to the surface.

The Titanic

The liner was built to carry 2,500 passengers in luxury—facilities included a gym, swimming pool, and Turkish baths. At the time, experts believed that the ship was unsinkable.

Learning from shipwrecks

Old ships do not normally survive. Their hulls rot away or are taken apart for salvage. This means that much of our knowledge of ancient ships comes from pictures or early descriptions. Archaeologists are therefore fascinated by shipwrecks. A shipwreck is like a time capsule. When a ship goes down, it takes with it a complete record of life on board. Underwater conditions can preserve ship timbers and other objects that would normally rot. They can give archaeologists invaluable information about hull construction, guns, masts, cargo, and the daily lives of sailors that they would not have been able to discover in any other way.

Glossary

aft Toward the rear, or stern, of the ship.

anchor A weighted structure used for mooring a vessel.

bireme An ancient warship powered by two banks of oars on each side of the hull, or frame, of the ship.

bowsprit A strong wooden beam that sticks out from the front of a sailing ship, used to attach rigging for forward sails.

bridge The raised area where a ship's captain stands, steers, and gives orders.

broadside Attack in which all the cannons on one side of a warship are fired at once.

bulkheads Walls that divide the ship into watertight compartments.

caravel A light sailing ship common in the Mediterranean in the 1400s and early 1500s.

chart A map of the sea, showing coasts, currents, islands, and other features.

chronometer A highly accurate clock which keeps precise time at sea and is used to help in navigation. The first chronometer was made by English clockmaker, John Harrison.

clinker-built Wooden ships built with the planks overlapping, like the clapboards of a house.

clipper A fast ship with a large sail, popular for carrying cargo long distances during the 1800s.

cog A large, medieval, square-sailed ship used for war and carrying cargo.

compass A navigation instrument that uses magnetism to point north. It was more reliable than the sun compass.

container ship A vessel designed to carry cargo containers of a standard size.

dinghy A small, open boat.

Dreadnought Class of powerful battleships of the early 1900s, named after a British ship with this name.

factory ship A fishing vessel equipped with facilities for cleaning, filleting, and freezing its catch.

fire ship A vessel deliberately set on fire and left to drift among an enemy fleet; used in warfare in the 1500s.

Galleon

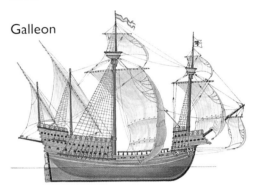

fore Toward the front of a ship.

forecastle Forward, raised part of a ship, often used for the crew's quarters.

frigate A term used at different times for several types of vessels. In the 1700s and 1800s, a frigate

Destroyer

carrack A large Mediterranean sailing ship used for both cargo and warfare; it was popular with explorers in the 1400s.

carvel-built Wooden ships built with the planks fixed together to prevent overlapping.

catamaran A lightweight boat with twin hulls to give it extra stability.

corsair A pirate or privateer, especially from the Mediterranean or France.

destroyer Traditionally, a small, fast-moving battleship, although the term is now used for modern battleships of a range of sizes and functions.

dhow A lateen-sailed vessel used widely in the Arab world.

was a medium-sized sailing ship, with square sails. In the United States, the Navy uses the term for a small escort ship, while in modern Britain, a frigate is usually a warship smaller than a destroyer.

galleon A large sailing ship, built high at fore and aft and used in warfare in the 1400s and 1500s, especially by the Spanish.

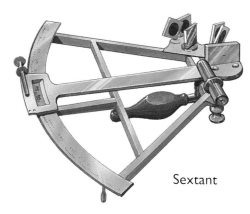

Sextant

galley A long ship, popular in the navies of the ancient world, powered by both oars and sails. It was developed by the Phoenicians.

hold The areas below deck where cargo is stored.

ironclad A ship powered by steam engines, with a hull protected by iron plates.

Jolly Roger A pirate flag, usually consisting of a white skull and crossbones on a black background.

junk A flat-bottomed sailing ship from eastern Asia, rigged with square sails which are usually supported by thin wooden battens.

keel The "backbone" of a ship running along the bottom of the ship from fore to aft.

knot A unit of speed at sea—one nautical mile per hour. It equals just over one mile per hour.

lateen The term used to describe a triangular sail.

latitude The distance from the equator. Lines of latitude run around the earth, parallel with the equator.

liner A large passenger-carrying ship run by a shipping company or line, usually offering luxury accommodations.

longitude The distance, measured in degrees, east or west of a line running through Greenwich, England. Lines of longitude run in great circles around the earth, passing through the poles.

man-of-war A large sailing warship of the 1700s and 1800s.

merchant ship A vessel used for carrying cargo.

oceanography The scientific study of the ocean.

orlop deck The lowest deck on a ship having four or more decks.

pilot A sailor with detailed knowledge of the local coast, who helps guide ships into port.

privateer A person or ship authorized to rob or seize an enemy's ships.

propeller A shaft, formed in the shape of a spiral, turned by the engine to drive a ship.

rigging The network of ropes that help holds up a ship's masts and allows the sails to be controlled.

rudder A large flat structure that is turned to steer a vessel and is attached by hinges to the rear of a ship.

scurvy A disease of the skin and gums caused by lack of vitamin C. It was discovered in the 1700s that eating plenty of fresh fruit and vegetables prevents it.

Tanker

sextant A navigational instrument used to measure the height of the sun from the horizon, enabling sailors to work out a ship's latitude.

stern The rear part of a vessel.

tanker A large ship that contains tanks to carry bulk liquids such as oil.

torpedo A self-propelled weapon, designed to travel under water, carrying an explosive charge that goes off when it hits its target.

trireme An ancient warship powered by three banks of oars on each side of the hull.

turbine engine An engine containing a wheel with vanes that turns as a result of pressure from water or steam.

yard A crossbar, mounted at right angles to a mast, which supports a sail.

Paddle steamer

Index

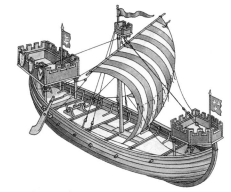

Acknowledgments

The publishers would like to thank the following
illustrators for their contributions to this book:

b = bottom, c = center, l = left, r = right, t = top, m = middle

Susanna Addario 43 *tr*; **Marion Appleton** 44 *c*; **Mark Bergin** 1 *c*, 3 *l*, 36–37, 37 *t*, 38–39;
Harry Bishop 54 *b*, 55 *t*; **Peter Bull** 6–7; **Gino D'Achille** 21 *t*, 21 *cl*, 58–59; **Mike Davis** 35 *tl*, 38 *t*;
Peter Dennis 14–15, 16–17, 17 *tr*; **Ed Dovey** 40–41; **Richard Draper** 16 *b*; **Chris Forsey** 10 *tl*, 10 *cr*;
Christian Hook 17 *br*; **Roy Huxley** 37 *c*, 39 *tr*; **John James** 8–9, 13, 36 *tl*, 42; **Kevin Maddison** 8 *tr*, 11, 24–25,
46–47, 56 *t*; **Chris Molan** 20–21, 34–35, 45, 48–49; **Roger Payne** 54 *tl*; **Peter Ross** 44 *tr*; **Kevan Rush** 3 *t*, 22 *t*;
Rodney Shakell 45 *tl*; **Mike Taylor** 12 *tl*; **Thomas Trojer** 28–29.

The publishers would also like to thank the following
for supplying photographs for this book:

b = bottom, c = center, l = left, r = right, t = top

Pages: **2** *br* The Bridgeman Art Library/Louvre, Paris, France; **3** *br* The Bridgeman Art Library/Bonhams, London;
4–5 Virgil Pomfret/Roger Desoutter; **10** *cl* Giraudon; **12** *tr* The Bridgeman Art Library/Metropolitan Museum
of Art, New York; **14** *tl* Mary Evans Picture Library/Explorers Archives; **15** *tr* The Bridgeman Art Library/British
Library, London; **18** *bl* National Maritime Museum Picture Library; **18–19** Virgil Pomfret/Roger Desoutter; **19** *t* The
Bridgeman Art Library/Natural History Museum, London, *tl* The Art Archive/British Museum, *tr* The Art Archive;
22 *cr* Corbis/Bettmann, *bl* The Bridgeman Art Library/National Maritime Museum; **22–23** *c* Virgil Pomfret/Roger
Desoutter; **23** *tr* Corbis; **25** *tr* Kos Picture Source Ltd./David Williams; **26** *tr* U.S. Navy; **29** *b* The Bridgeman Art
Library/Musée de la Tapisserie, Bayeux, France; **30** *tr* The Mary Rose Trust, *b* AKG London/Archivio Cameraphoto
Venezia; **34** *tr* The Bridgeman Art Library/Private Collection, *c* The Art Archive/De Vries; **35** *tr* The Bridgeman Art
Library/Roderick Lovesey/David Messum Gallery, London (we have been unable to trace the copyright holder and
would be grateful to receive any information as to their identity); **38** *b* U.S. Navy; **43** *br* "Courtesy of the Pilgrim
Society, Plymouth, Massachusetts"/Bacon; **46** *tr* Corbis; **47** *tr* Science & Society Picture Library/Science Museum;
48 *tr* Peter Newark's Pictures; **49** *tr* Corbis/Bettmann, *cr* The Bridgeman Art Library/Victoria & Albert Museum,
London (we have been unable to trace the copyright holder and would be grateful to receive any information as to
their identity); **50** *cr* The Advertising Archive; *br* Science & Society Picture Library/National Railway Museum; **50–51** *t*
Princess Cruises; **51** *br* Virgil Pomfret/Roger Desoutter; **55** *br* Michael Holford; **56** *cl* Corbis; *c* Corbis; **57** *c* Corbis, *br*
National Maritime Museum Picture Library; **58** *tr* Corbis; **59** *t* Corbis, *c* The Art Archive/Dennis Cochrane Collection.

Every effort has been made to trace the copyright holders of the photographs.
The publishers apologize for any inconvenience caused.